Zak and Zee

Jeanne Willis ✳ Mark Oliver

OXFORD

UNIVERSITY PRESS

In this story

Zak Bug

Zee Bug

Two green bugs sat in a tree.
One was Zak and one was Zee.

Zak had big, big, yellow eyes ...
... bigger than a dragonfly's.

Zee Bug's eyes were very small.
He did not see well at all.

Zee saw a bug.

He called out, "Hi!"

The other bug did not reply.

"Oh," Zee said, "I wonder why?
Why that bug does not reply."

"Maybe he just did not hear."
So Zee shouted in his ear.

"Would you like to come to tea?
Come and have some tea
with me."

Still the bug did not reply.
So Zee had another try.

"Would you like to come to tea?
Come and have some tea
with me."

"That's my tail!" Zak softly said.
Zee turned very, very red.

"My eyes are on my face," said Zak.
"You keep talking to my back."

"I do not see well, it's true.
But I can fly as well as you."

The two bugs flew away to play. Zak's eyes helped them find their way.